# THE

## SHE BECAME

PART I

# THE

## *Woman*

# SHE BECAME

## PART I

SAPPHIRE

**The Woman She Became - Part I**

Names, locations and most importantly, some timelines have been changed and/ or omitted to protect the true identities of characters introduced in this book. Every reference and similarity to actual events, real people, living or dead, are intended and not coincidental. However, this is my story in my own words, told solely by me.

Book Cover and Design by: oliviaprodesign

ISBN: 978-1-7355315-0-2
First Edition: August 2020
10 9 8 7 6 5 4 3 2 1

"I'm not trying to sell you a story,
I'm tryna tell you my truth!"

*SAPPHIRE*

# CONTENTS

## Life Chapters 0-10

## Life Chapters 11-20

# ACKNOWLEDGEMENTS

First and foremost, I would like to thank God. Every day was a struggle and I thank you for allowing me to stay focused.

The Universe, for energy and clarity.

My Princesses, my daughters, A'Janae and Tier'Ney, thank you for the unconditional love and support you give and show me daily. You are the reason I continue to push through to my goals. Thank you for understanding.

FAB 4… Yvette, Aisha, and Buffy! What can I say? This friendship has been truly motivating. You ladies hold me accountable for my words, actions, and decisions. You keep me honest and on a straight and narrow. Thank you for the motivation and the counseling even when you did not know. I've learned so much from this friendship… from the trips, the infamous round table talks, the conference calls, the fasting and praying, the touching and agreeing, through the good, the bad, the happy and the sad… our bond is amazing and I will cherish it always.

#4, thank you for keeping me on track and making sure I met my deadlines. For proofreading, editing, and answering all of my questions in the middle of night. Thank you for the motivation, the support, and the talks. Thank you for EVERYTHING!

Dunlap Clan… #1-Dee-Dee, #2-Tivia, #3-Tammy, #4- Cherry, #5-Kaloa, #6-Pete Dun-Leap, #8-Vette, and #9-Nellie, thank you all for the motivation. From the *early* "good morning" texts to the yearly get togethers whenever I can make it home. I love you guys so much and I look to you for guidance and your continued love and support. Thank you for all of that and so much more!

To Calvin… You have no idea how you have motivated me. I have learned so much from you. Thank you for understanding and knowing the difference when I needed to just be alone and when I needed to just lay in your arms. Keep your head up, stay the course and all your dreams will come true. Most importantly, know that I got your back!

To my Dunlap, Whitehurst, and Berrien family (those who claim me as family), I love you… Forever!

To you, yes you who is currently reading and have purchased this book, thank you for the love and support!

## DEDICATION

To my mother, Stella L. Dunlap, you taught me to be a free spirit and at a very young age I have been telling you that all I wanted to do was write, not formal, but in my own way. You supported me and encourage me to go after my dreams. And although you are not here to hold the book in your hands and read it (which is probably a good thing), I know you are here with me every day in spirit. I thank you for gracing me with your spirit when I needed that extra push. I love you momma and I miss you so much! I will continue to be true to who I am and the woman you raised me to be!

To my father, my daddy, Wille L. Dunlap, II better known as Pete, if it were not for you, I would not be here. Thank you for being the best daddy you know to be. Thank you for stepping up when momma passed. We all forget that at one point she was the love of your life and you were hurting just as much, if not more than us. Thank you for being selfless and encouraging. Thank you for opening your world up to me and my daughters. I appreciate the effort you continue to make. Stay strong in your journey… You Got This! I love you daddy!

To all the women (and men) out there that have ever been through something or that is going through something right now and suppressed or is suppressing it because you were/are afraid of how the world would see you. This book is dedicated to you; be inspired, tell your story, free yourself, and get the release you have been longing for. It is your time to shine!

*SAPPHIRE*

Life

Chapters

0-10

*SAPPHIRE*

# "STRUCTURED LIFE"

In order to tell you who she became, I first have to let you know who she was, where she come from and what she has been through. First, let me just clarify that "she" is ME!

Have you ever sat still and thought about your life? Like, if it would have been different if certain things did not happen? Well, that is a constant thought of mine and I can't seem to get the thought out of my head. Growing up in a house full, it was always

3

something going on. I had a great childhood, for the most part. My mother did her best with what she had. She birthed 8 children, 7 girls and a boy. Yes, she was busy… I guess there was no color tv back then. My mother had asthma and was sick for as long as I could remember, so my older sisters did a lot for us younger siblings. They basically took care of us. They did our hair, made sure we cleaned the house, cooked for us until we were tall enough to reach the stove. At that point we had to learn how to cook. Everyone had a day to cook, my day was Thursdays. My favorite meal back then was rice, cream-style corn, and fried spam, and that is what I cooked for the family every Thursday evening. You couldn't tell me nothing… I was a chef! LOL. We all had a specific time for everything. Dinner needed to be at a certain time to leave enough time for the person that had to clean the kitchen to be done by 9pm… because that was bedtime. And we were never late for bedtime because we had a reminder. See, we lived in front of railroad tracks and like clockwork, you would hear the train's horn at approximately 9pm… bedtime! Oh yeah… everyone had an area to clean on a weekly rotation basis. I think this is when I developed OCD. We had a routine for everyday… Sundays, my mother or one of my older sisters would wake up early, turn on that good old school gospel music and make breakfast while we got ready. After breakfast we would go to Sunday School, 11am service, and if there was an afternoon service, we were there! We were raised to go to church every time the doors open! When we got home, we would eat Sunday dinner as a family, then start ironing clothes for the school week, and like clockwork bedtime at 9pm. Our schedule was as follows, Mondays-Fridays, go to school, come home, cook, clean, bed at 9pm, except on Fridays, we stayed up until 10pm. Saturdays- spring cleaning day… we would wake up early to thoroughly clean the entire house, wash clothes and get our hair combed (I hated getting my hair combed-it hurt), then we were sent to play OUTSIDE (this is where

6

our heads would be on fire from the grease on our scalps). We would eat (dinner was whatever left over from the week), clean, get clothes (dress or blouse and skirt) ready for Sunday, (females wearing pants were frown upon back then) … and bed at 9pm.

One thing I can say about my childhood, it was structured for sure. We did a lot of playing outside because we couldn't be amongst the grown-ups. The kids remained kids and stayed in a kid's place. We were not allowed to just sit and talk with the adults, that was unheard of at 309! And if you are thinking of asking, YES, we got whoopings! My mother did NOT spare the rod to spoil us! If we did something, she would talk to us first and then tell us why she was going to whoop us. And when they say, "it takes a village", back then it did. Your neighbors were "the village", who, if they saw you acting up could and would punish you and then call your mother so that when you get home, you'd have another one coming. This would make any kid want to do right while in the community. I'm not saying that it was right or wrong, but I think I turned out to be a well-rounded, respectful woman with a good head on my shoulders and for the most part, my siblings too are thriving and doing well.

# "MY FIRST CRUSH"

It was in the first grade when I first noticed him. Mrs. Durrance was my teacher. I cannot remember if he was in my class or not. You couldn't tell me nothing. I had a major crush on this boy, and I was gonna make him my boyfriend. I didn't know how because I was so shy back then. I know that is hard to believe but it's true! Anyway, I do not remember when he approached me, but we ended up calling ourselves boyfriend and girlfriend. He would come all the way to my house to play with me, my sisters and brother. We had so much fun just hanging out. Because back then, nothing physical was going on… I was a virgin and I planned to stay that way until marriage. At least that was the planned. And I almost made it, but you would have to finish reading to find out what/who took me off course.

It was gross to do anything but hold hands, and even that was pushing it. It was a major step forward in our relationship. After a few years or so of us being together we had to get married! LOL… and we did! We had a ceremony in my mother's backyard, he gave me one of them fake play ring. When I tell

10

you that I was in heaven, it was the most exciting day of my life! The fact that he would walk all the way to my house every day to come and see me so we could all play outside meant everything. We became the best of friends. He lived across the highway, which was far to us as kids. We had so much fun, so innocent, kids being kids, playing house and holding hands. He would have to come and see me because we couldn't go anywhere. My mother was a true protector, so we were not allowed to go to many places without our older sisters. Which I didn't understand back then, but I do now.

Where I am from the Elementary School was K-3, Riverside was 4-5, Middle School was 6-7, and High School was 8-12. Now, this has changed since I was in school. When we were ending our time at Riverside, which is still elementary for most schools, and entering Middle School, my "husband" and I broke up, although we remained best friends. It was known that we would always be an item and we would not seriously entertain anyone else. Well that shit went down the drain when my uncle moved here with his family and my first cousin expressed interest in him. Me being me, I was honest and told her that he was off limits, but we do not go together anymore, and he is single, but he is taken. I know… confusing. But I meant exactly what I said! I guess she took it as a joke and she approached him and just like that, they started going together. When I got word about it, I was done with both of them! Like I said, he was supposed to have been my husband when we got grown, but that was out the window. Ain't NO way I was going to get back with him after he decided to entertain her. Even though nothing physically happened between them at this time, I thought that was just nasty. She instantly became the enemy and he was just on the "do not talk to" list. Only because this boy has been my best friend for years now and it was easier to not talk to him. Hell, I didn't know her! She was my first cousin, but we had just met. And at this point I did not want and was not going to bother trying to get to know her. She was irrelevant because she violated family code and she wasn't to be trusted! "Fuck her!" That was my answer to any and everyone who asked me about that situation. I did not talk to her for the longest and I was fine without her in my life. I literally did not forgive her for what she did until we were fully grown. I am at the point now where I can see her, speak to her and be okay with it. I had to keep telling myself, "In order to move on you must forgive. Forgiveness is for you, not for the other person."

After a while, I was able to speak to my best friend. I did not care what the situation was, he should not have broken our bond. He should have been stronger than that. But then again when I think back on it, he was a little horny teenager and was after anything and every girl that moved, soooooo I understood, I guess! I didnt care anymore; I was happy to have my best friend back. Not as a boyfriend though, just strictly friends. We talked about everything; we still do! He is straightforward with me and I with him. We have never held back our thoughts from each other, whether it hurt feelings or not. We let each other have it, bluntly and wholeheartedly. The friendship we have now is unmatched. In the end, I am okay with how things went down because I don't think that we would be this close if it had gone any other way. "I definitely dodged a bullet with breaking it off with him back then!"

# "LOST INNOCENCE"

When a little girl has her innocence taken away from her, her life changes forever! Summers in Florida were always fun… until they were not! I used to love going to different cities to stay with family, to hang with cousins. I used to be this bubbly little tomboy without a worry in the world. I would rather play with the boys because the girls did not want to be outside… I was and still am an outside chick.

This particular summer, it was decided that we would not all go visit family at the same time, it would be me and my twin sister and my sister and brother (who were also twins) would split the summer equally. Oh yeah, I forgot to tell you that my mother had two sets of twins, identical and fraternal. Anyway, this particular summer my twin sister and I went first. We were so excited to go and spend time with all of our cousins. We were to be there for two weeks and then the other set of twins would go the following two weeks. I don't remember if they went or not, because any and everything that happened after our first night there was a complete blur.

When we got there, we were told where we would be sleeping for the duration of our time there and where to put our things. My cousin gave us a tour of the house. It was beautiful just like her. I knew we were raised in the same manner because her house was immaculate. I think she had a case of OCD too. After we put our things up, we all were in the living watching tv and talking about what we were going to do the next day. I do not remember my cousin leaving to go to bed as me and my sister fell asleep on the living room floor. It was that first night, I felt a tap and then a voice say, "if you tell, I will deny it, and nobody will believe you". I am thinking to myself, "tell what?" And then it happened, he pulled my pajamas down and commence to molesting me. I didn't know what to do. I was scared to move. I didn't make the slightest of sound because I did not want to get in trouble. After an unknown amount of time passes of violation, he stopped and got up. I didn't know where he went because my eyes were closed the entire time. I was ashamed, I didn't know if my twin sister was awake or not. I couldn't bear the thought of her seeing me in that condition or having knowledge that this happened, and she tell, and nobody believes neither one of us. I was no longer a kid; my innocence was gone, taken… lost! …and I could not get it back. I was damaged goods and no man would ever want me. These are the thoughts that are going through my mind as he is bouncing up and down on me. With tears flowing from my eyes, he sees them, but they have no impact on him at all. The next day, he is acting as if nothing happened, as if he didn't just change my whole life!

After that first night, I had it in my mind that we would not sleep in the living room. So, I made sure that the moment I felt sleepy, I would go to the bedroom.

Thinking that this was just a one-time thing I went on with our trip as planned, not saying nothing to nobody, about last night, not even my twin sister. I made sure the following night my sister and I would go to the room that was prepared for us, close the door, and go to sleep. And then without missing a beat, the tap came and those words again… and so did the tears. Again, the bouncing, still he was not phased at all by the tears now coupled with sniffling. He did not care that my twin sister was in the bed next to me, he did his business and got up like nothing happened. The next day same as the day before, he acted as if he did not do anything. This happened for the next several days… My sister and I cried and begged to be taken home, that we were missing home too much and would like to cut our trip short.

When we got home, nothing was said, and nothing was suspected. I unpacked and went about my life as if everything were just grand. I never said a word to anyone! And for years I suppressed it. Knowing on the inside I was dying and there was nothing nobody could do about it.

It was as if it never happened, but it would impact me for the rest of my life. The "what-if's", and the "why me" hunts me daily. I was only ten years old! Why would someone do that to a ten-year-old! I was seventy pounds soak and wet with clothes on, I was so tiny and petite. I was not even fully developed yet! "Why?" "Just why?"

There is nothing in this world that can trouble you more than your own thoughts. "Does anyone else find it crazy that you can be so fucking depressed that no one around you ever notice? NO ONE! Like you can literally be on the verge of drowning in your own tears and everyone is totally oblivious!" This has single handedly ruin my life! And from where I stood, I had no reason to live. I was only ten and I am thinking about ending it all! Only if I knew how to carry it out… However, if I did, I wouldn't be here today to tell my story! And if I could put it into words the way I felt… "Lost, hurt and abandon".

Everything we go through I believe we go through it for a reason. But with everything in me I have yet to find the reason this happened to me. It has broken my trust and faith in humans. This has affected the way I deal with men, the way I accept them and how I allow them to interact with me in my life. I have put up so many mental walls that I sometimes think that I have a hard time getting to and through to myself. It has just been really difficult getting past this.

"I've learned not to trust people, including family. I've learned not to believe what they say, but to watch what they do. I've learned to suspect that any and everyone is capable of living a lie. And most importantly, I've come to believe that people, even when you think you know them, and they are family are ultimately unknowable."

Life

Chapters

11-20

*SAPPHIRE*

## "YOUNG AND NOT SO READY"

It was after school when I was asked to come over to a friend's house. We had met about a week or so before. He was older and much more mature than me. I am not usually interested in someone my own age, I would rather a much older gentleman. Not sure if this had anything to do with what happened to me, but this was my preference now. Well, I went over there, having to sneak away, because my mother would never allow me to go over to a boy's house, especially when their mother isn't home. As we were watching tv, he started touching and feeling all over me. We started kissing. In that moment I really didn't know it was gonna end up with him trying to have intercourse with me. To me, I was still a baby because I had never had consensual sex before. And I did not even know what to do. My body tense up! Not allowing him to enter, although he tried. It was not happening. After about a few minutes of trying, I got up and left, embarrassed and ashamed, thinking something was definitely wrong with me. We probably talked for a day or so after that and then never said another word to each other, but "hey" when we saw each other in the streets.

After that incident, my spirit was broken, and I just knew I would never find a guy who I would be comfortable and free enough with to relax and just let it happen with. And then out of nowhere this guy approached me. He was a fine specimen of a man, sexy in his own right and I was very attracted to him. He was fun to be around, and I was really comfortable with him. I decided to take it slow with this one, therefore it took a while before I would see him in a private setting. He seemed to be ok with it and that made me appreciate him even more, which in turn allowed me to let down my guard with him.

He was gentle and patient. Although we were alone, we kissed and guess what? It didn't lead to anything! I was so pleasantly surprised and grateful. He told me that I was worth waiting for. This guy was a complete gentleman. We got along great; the only thing was I just was not into him like that. I saw him more as a close friend. Someone who I could get a man's point of view from. After having that conversation with him, he all of a sudden did not want to hang out anymore and told me that he cannot just be my friend. I did understand but I didn't want to lose him as a friend. This was my life for the next couple of guys I met. Until one day, I decided to just stop trying. I had given up on men, marriage… everything! "Is it because of what

happened to me when I was ten"

## "FOCUSED AND OFF LIMITS"

All in the world was going as planned. I was in school, focused on schoolwork as I strived to be on the honor roll list. Enjoying life, being a normal teenager and focusing on my only goals. See, I was in my second and last year of middle school and I kept myself pretty busy. I buried myself into my schoolwork to stay out of trouble. The past few years were not so great. Although I had my best friend back in my life, I did not look at boys quite the same anymore. I did not want to have anything to do with any of them. I had no worries and no commitments to anyone. Free as a bird to do exactly what I wanted, well to do as my mother expected of me. I was the model student, but most importantly, a good daughter. Trying not to get in trouble, which a lot of you reading this who know me knows very well that that is something that is extremely hard for me because of my mouth. I promise I am doing better though. Just continue praying for me.

Anyway, as I focus on my goals, it made me give less attention to other things. My walls started to become invisible because there was no need for them as I was not even looking for anything in that department. Well, what I did not know was, just because I was not looking does not mean that there were not folks out there that was not preying and looking to take advantage of me. I did not know how far and wide those walls stretched until I was vulnerable to another act of selfishness.

Yes! I thought for sure that certain people I should not have to question their character. It has already been approved. Their loyalty and trust, people that I have seen over a thousand times in my home with family and friends, people I called family have already been vetted by my loved ones. Right?!?! Wrong! This individual I knew as family took advantage of me in a way I would not have ever thought. As I answered a knock at the door, I was forcefully thrown on the couch, as I fought back with all my might, and before I could ask, "what are you doing?", he tore my panties right off me and commenced to ripping into me… I could not believe it! I was in excruciating pain… I was screaming at the top of my lungs. But no one was home. See, this person said that he was just stopping by to drop something off for my mother and that she knew he was coming by. Of course, my mother did not know I was home, let along home alone. On this day, I had got sick and was not feeling well so I left school early. I wrote a letter, stating that I had a doctor's appointment and that my mother would be outside waiting on me. Letter was signed so my mother did not actually have to be present. I left and went home. The house was quiet, so I went straight to my room and went to sleep. Usually my momma is home, but for some reason, she was not there. Nobody was there! It was kind of weird, but I am not usually there during the day. I remember everything about that day, from the cologne he was wearing, to the clothes he was wearing. And he had the nerves to throw money at me... on the same couch he threw me on to do what he really came to do. He got up as if nothing he just did was completely and utterly wrong. When he had his pants back up, he leaned over to whisper in my ear, "if you say anything to anyone, especially your mother, I will kill you!" I am only twelve years old! I was terrified. I knew that my mother would probably take him out at the thought of it but did not know what kind of war it would cause in the community or if I would be believed. I could not risk my mother's life. I was devastated... AGAIN! I didn't have no choice but to keep quiet and forget it ever happen... Suppressed!

And just like that I was back into my shell, my "safe" place. I really don't like men, at all! I hate them! I cannot stand certain smells of soap and cologne because it reminds me of when I was ten and this moment. It is not a game; this shit is real, and it is extremely hard to cope with when you are terribly afraid to talk to anyone about it. "This can't be life!" The folks that we call family should be protecting, not harming me. It was in that moment; my trust became nonexistent for everyone! I did not care who you were, I was questioning everything! I started to lose friends, not because they did not like me, but because I didn't make myself friendly. It was just easier for me to be by myself. I could cope better if I didn't feel like I needed to open up to anyone and it happens to slip out. I wasn't ready to die, at least not by someone else's hands.

I did what I did best… I lost myself in my schoolwork. I realized in that moment that there are really some evil people in this world… and from what I have experienced, they were all a part of my family in some way, shape or form. And some people say, family is all we got. Well, if that is the case, I don't want it! And if I believe that then I ain't got shit! Because the family that I know did not have a problem harming me. "You can't protect that which you have harmed." Experiences have taught me that trust is earned and not freely given, that loyalty is not in the forefront of everyone's mind and heart, and family don't always have your best interest at heart and can at any time mentally and physically harm you.

## "THEY MEET"

M y first year of high school I started playing volleyball. It is a sport that a few of my sisters played while in high school. Being the younger sister always looking up to my older sisters, I followed in their footsteps. I had to keep my mind from wandering to the past and focused on the now. Volleyball became the only reason for me to live, literally. I was good at it too, and I wanted to one day play for a college, but that dream came to a screeching halt.

After my first year in high school, which started in 8th grade, I realized that volleyball was my saving grace and that is what I will focus on to get me out of my little town. It was after a home volleyball game when he asked me if I wanted a ride home. I quickly said, "No!" First of all, "Who are you?", but I already knew exactly who he was, and not at all interested in getting to know him. The next day, after I got home from school he ended up at my house. I was at the dining room table doing my homework when I heard a knock at the door. I was like, "How can I help you?" He said that he wanted to "talk" to me. I asked, "About what?" He said that his cousin said that I told him that he was cute, which I did, but that doesn't mean that I wanted that message to get to him. I said, "I did, but that's it!" He was like, "Well I think you're cute too." I said, "Thank you". I was about to shut the door when my mother came out of her room and asked who he was. He introduced himself because I had no intentions of introducing him… I was not interested in him staying as long as he has stayed already. This was getting really uncomfortable for me and it was way too much for me to process. He sat and talked with my mother for a while, I guess expressing his interest in me. Once my mother made her rules clear, he turned to me and was trying to talk. I talked for a minute

SAPPHIRE

or so and then I was like, ok… we can try this out. I had zero faith in whatever this was and no intention of a future with this guy. He did ask if he could come and pick me up to take me to and from school. That was different and the fact that I wouldn't have to ride the bus was a great trade off. He didn't go to my school, nor did he live in the same town as me. So, to me this was a hell of a commitment.

He was actually a nice guy. A total gentleman, and you can tell he was raised by a strong black woman. He was older, three years older than me and born in the same month as me. All these qualities were adding up. He was becoming cuter and cuter by the

46

day... LOL! We started hanging out every day... he was growing on me. We would go to the movies, dinner, and just ride around and talk or hang out at my house, watching tv and talking about any and everything. Day by day he was breaking through my mental barriers and tearing those walls down. The more we hung out, the more comfortable and freer I was around him. I am not sure how long it was before he had me open and willing to say and do anything. I have never felt this freeing spirit with or around any other guy before, except my best friend. It was something different about this guy and I wanted to know more. It was like it was always something new, although it really was

47

not but it seemed that way. He made me forget about everything negative that had happened to me. We did not talk about it at this early stage because I did not want to scare him off. This was my time and I felt that God had heard my prayers and sent him to me. Even though I was not in love, I really like this guy. He was taking time out of his life to spend with me. I mean a lot of his time. I needed to appreciate him for that.

Now that I am an open book to this man, he couldn't say or do no wrong. He was very expressive and did not hold back on how he was starting to feel about me and neither did I. We decide that we would commit and get into a relationship. This was a huge deal for me, but like I said, he made me feel comfortable. My relationships before him, they both cheated. He would be different for sure. He was more mature, older, and more experienced.

We did move fast. One reason is because I thought I was way behind the curb because I had sworn off men at such an early age. And all of my teammates were already in relationships. Within several months we have decided to take our relationship to the next level past the kissing stage. You guys know me now, and you know that this is a major step for me, and I am terrified. Scared of my reaction to the act, scared that it would not work because I would not open up to him and "she" would reject him. I did not know what was going to happen, but we were about to see. One thing we did not talk about was kids, because I did not want any, at least not yet anyway. He never stopped the gestures and we still spent quite a bit of time together. However, after we did get physical, I noticed a minor change. He was not as available and I could tell that he was sharing the time he used to spend with me, somewhere else. We as women, we have this thing called intuition. Which at this time I had no idea what it was, I just knew I had the feeling something wasn't quite right.

During this time, I met his mother and stepfather… I fell in love with them both.

And when he took me around the rest of his family I felt right at home. Even though I was shy and did not talk much at first, I was still comfortable around them. They quickly gained my trust and they became my family. I still have love for them. I built a few bonds and real friendships. A few of his cousins became like sisters to me and we still talk. I cherish our friendship and would not change it for the world.

When the rumors of him entertaining other females started and finally got back to me, I was not surprised. I turned my focused back to volleyball, but as I said earlier it had to come to a screeching halt... because unbeknownst to me and him, while I had played most of that season, I was with child. I had no idea and did not notice that my attitude had changed. My mother was the one that told me that I was pregnant, and I needed to go to the clinic for a checkup. He took me and her statement was true, and I was indeed pregnant. My mother knew her child! I was not happy and never thought for one second of doing anything other than taking care of it. My first thought was I got to get my life together so that I can move out of my mother's house. She was already struggling to take care of us and here I am about to bring another mouth in here for her to feed. I could not and would not be ok with that. But my mother being who she is was like "You don't have to leave; we will make it work." My momma was the absolute best! And at the tender age of fifteen, still in high school, not old enough to sign for my own place, I had someone else sign for me an apartment. I moved out of my mother's house, mentally but ALL of my belongings were still there…

I even had the baby's crib put up in my room that I shared with my twin sister. I was not ready physically to leave the fold. I had an apartment, but I can count on one hand how many nights I stayed there while pregnant. But it was there just in case. I did not know how these hormones may have me acting and my momma would kick me out before she killed me. That I was appreciative of, LOL…

I am laughing but my momma was crazy and did not care who knew it. That is another reason my secrets were kept secrets because those punks from my childhood would have met their maker sooner rather than later.

Anyway, just so you guys are clear on how serious I was about this volleyball thing, I vowed to keep playing until I started showing or the game became too physical where it was putting my baby at risk. The latter happened. I was cleared by my doctor to continue to do all activities that I was doing before I got pregnant. I was digging and diving for balls, and my teammates were worried. See, I only told a few of my classmates and teammates, because I felt they needed to know since we played on the same team. I had to do something that would change my world again… I had to quit the game that brought me back to life, that gave me the motivation I needed to press on. Now I was at a crossroads and needed another motivation. I was known as a happy person before I got pregnant and that did not change. What I expressed was happiness because nobody would be able to understand the shit that was going on in my mind. I had a live person growing inside of me and a dude in my life who is doing only God knows what with God knows who. I had no motivation or hope to carry on… so much going on.

As if it couldn't get any worst, one day I started feeling a sharp pain in my side. All day at school… I was feeling this pain. I didn't say anything because it was so early, and my baby was not ready to be born. I thought it was something that I ate. When I got home, I jumped in the shower and laid down. Later that night, my twin sister asked me what was wrong, and I told her that I was feeling pain in my side, she was not as calm. She jumped up and went and told my momma. Her being our protector rushed me to the hospital and it was there when I realized that mothers are always right. I had pneumonia. They immediately admitted me and transferred me to ICU. Where I could have only three people in my room at a time. Now, that was going to be a problem. My immediate family is huge and then you have his family. It was the scariest thing I had ever been through. I was just a baby; I was carrying a baby and it was my responsibility to make sure that my baby will be ok. While in the hospital the entire right side of my body shut down, all of my organs, my lung, my kidney… it was hard for me to breath and with every movement I was gasping for air. I could not do anything for myself. I remember one of my sisters had to bath me, she would come and visit me every day to make sure I was clean for any visitors that came to see me, even if it was just my immediate family who was allowed to see me. I remember being in there for a while, and when I was discharged, I went back home with my momma... still was not ready to leave the fold.

My momma made sure I did not miss a beat when it came to school. She went to the school to make sure that I got all of my schoolwork for the days that were missed while in the hospital. When I was strong enough, I returned to school. I was happy and excited to get back to my regular routine.

My mother, sisters, and a cousin got together and planned a baby shower for me. I was grateful. I got more stuff than I could ever ask for. Both his family and mine supported me, and I love them for loving me through this journey as I am sure they were going through their own stuff.

Even though the dynamic of our relationship changed, at no time did I deny him of seeing or spending time with me while I was pregnant. I wanted him to experience this as well. I was not that type of girl. Even though my outlook on him had slightly change I could not deny him of this experience. This was a first for the both of us.

# "SHE'S GORGEOUS"

It was a regular day at school. My twin sister got sick and they called me to the office. I did not know what was going on, all I knew was that she had just thrown up. I had no pain, no pressure, I felt nothing! The school nurse advised me to go to the hospital because she believed that I was in labor. And sure enough, she was right. I went to the hospital where he met me. We walked up, they checked me in. The doctor checked me and said that I had dilated, and I would be having my baby before the night was over. And after the most trying but exciting nine months of my life, we welcomed a beautiful baby girl. She was perfect… I checked for two arms, two legs, ten fingers, and ten toes… then I checked facial to make sure she was as perfect as I knew she would be. And she was!

I tried to keep my newborn away from the public as much as possible. But folks will find a way to get a glimpse of the new kid on the block. There were folks coming to my mother's house that I didn't even know. I made sure that my daughter stayed in the back when there were company. I was really protective of her space. I mean, folks that didn't even talk to me was coming by to "check on me". I was not buying any of that. Everyone would have to wait until I was ready to bring her out. Her father came by every day. He was a hands-on daddy. I could not have asked for a better daddy for my daughter. His mother and stepfather were involved as well. This was their first grand baby.

It was towards the end of the school year when I gave birth and because high school is not set up to handle a pregnancy case, as I was one of the first cases at my high school. I couldn't take off the full six weeks' time required by my doctor. In order for me to graduate the following year, there were mandatory testing that I had to get done when scheduled. They were schedule the last weeks of the school year. I had only two weeks to recover as much as possible. As my MuDear would say, "You still stanking! You need to be home for at least six weeks." But I was not about to risk repeating the eleventh grade. So, I set up day care for my baby. I registered her at the same day care that I attended when I was a baby to toddler. Ms. Lola and her staff were the absolute best! They took great care of my princess. I was so blessed to be able to not have to worry about that part of her life. I was OCD with her too. Full body checks coming and going. I did not trust nobody with my baby out of my site. I did not want nothing to happen to her. She could not talk to tell me if something was wrong or if someone did something to her. It was not until she was able to talk that I would let her out of my site, but not for too long.

I had started going back to school, I was a senior now... with a child, so, I could not do everything everyone else was doing. I had responsibility and goals. And I needed to reach these goals, not only for me, but for my little person. I was exhausted, but I kept pushing. My family supported and helped me out a lot. My mother would come and get my baby in the middle of the night so that I could sleep through the night. At least that is what she told me, but I am sure she just wanted to spoil her. I was going to do whatever it took to make sure she did not go through the same stuff I had to go through growing up. I wanted to give her the world and in order to do that I had to remain focused. I started back playing volleyball. I just loved that sport. Kept me busy, but I could not keep up with it and take care of my daughter. Something had to give. Volleyball it was. My daughter needed to be raised and I was not about to let someone else raise her. So, I started putting in applications. I ended up getting a job at Hardee's.

During this time, he proposed to me... I was happy, until I was not!

One day, I open my locker at school and there was a letter in there addressed to me, from a distant cousin of mine. This letter was very explicit, detailing everything. I was upset, but not angry... if that make sense. I was upset because I did not think he would stoop this low to mess with my family, but I was not angry because I didn't put nothing passed anyone. Trust was out the door. He had broken so many promises that I was not going to let it affect me anymore. When I got home, to his house, I asked him about it and gave him the letter and of course, being in the same fashion as always, he told me that he didn't do nothing with her. Like I said, I was not mad because at this point, he had already

66

proved himself to be exactly who he was. And the fact that he sat up there with a straight face let me know that he was capable of anything. So, I just blew it off. Because at some point the truth will come out.

## "ADULTING, WHILE STILL A CHILD"

The ups and downs back and forth were getting redundant and old. Even though he was doing his part in helping me take care of her, he was not quite ready to settle down. He had some more mingling he wanted and needed to do. I went with the flow, because, well, I just did not know any better. That is the only way I can explain it, because I have no idea why I put up with any of it. But I did and I don't regret it. I am a believer of fairy tales and I just knew he would come to his senses and choose our daughter over these outside chickens. But he didn't. Every time he broke up with me, it wouldn't be a week before he would be calling me back telling me he's sorry. And I took him back every time. He used to start arguments with me so I would get mad and that would give him a reason to go out. I did not catch on to that until later on though.

About a year or so before this, he had purchased his first home. He said that it was for his family… him, me, and our daughter. But every time he got mad, he would kick me out and of course I would take our daughter with me. So, he would be left there alone. I figured that what he said about buying the house for the family was ultimately a lie and just another one of his ploys to get me back. Sometimes he would just get mad and leave, leaving us there for the night until he got back before day in the morning. This went on for several months extending over a year. I was still in high school and have not graduated yet. I was still working at Hardee's and my best friend's mother was the manager. One day, he got mad at me and did not want to take me to work. So, I called my best friend to take me. Of course, he was hesitant because my daughter's father thought that he and I had something going on because we were so close. But in reality, we really did not. But you couldn't tell him that. Well, right as my best friend was dropping me off at work, my daughter's father pulled up. He was angry, that I got a ride from someone else, especially him. He physically forced me into his car and drove me back to his house. Now, mind you, his house is in the next town over. So, I am away from my family and my daughter is at my mother's house, because I was supposed to be at work. I did not get a chance to call the manager so ultimately, I had to quit that job, because I knew I was fired for a no call, no show. I was upset! I had been working there a while and I was using this money to stack so that I can make a better living for me and my daughter. Instead, I am at his house. He is yelling and asking questions. I did not argue back because it was just a simple ride to work for me, nothing more. Mind you, he is out here doing whatever and with whoever. I have not said a word about nothing. Because to me, I was focused on my goal, which was getting out of that small town. After he did all of that arguing, he never apologized… he took me back to my mom's and left. But not before he broke up with me. I was cool because senior skip day was tomorrow!

Tomorrow was here, it was senior skip day! This was a day that all the seniors would skip school. On this day I was sick of the back and forth with him. I was sick of him accusing me of my best friend. I was gonna prove him right! So, I made plans to hang out with my best friend. When I got to his house, we did not do much talking. I was so focused on getting back at my daughter's father that I needed to make him feel exactly the way I felt every time I would hear about him being with another female. Not for him, for me! I wanted to see the hurt in his eyes when he asked me did anything happen between me and my best friend. So, we did the unthinkable. Call me what you want, but I was tired of hearing all this shit that he was doing with all these chicks. It all just came to a head, forgetting my vow when I was younger about my best friend being off limits because of my cousin, it went down. Right, wrong, or otherwise, it happened, and I cannot say that I regret it… but I definitely did not feel better after it happened. Although it was amazing and I enjoyed every bit of it, I would never do it again! I was still young, in high school… just out here on some "get back!" Even though my daughter's father and I was broken up, I still felt horrible. I could and would never again jeopardize me and my best friend's friendship for a physical moment… a moment when I was not in my right mind and in mental pain. Here is a moment we can never get back. It happened and now I am just as bad as my daughter's father.

He never asked about my day and I never said a word. He never apologized for the night before either. I guess things did not work out as he had planned the night before, because now, he wanted to have a talk. He wanted me to consider coming to live with him. I really wanted this relationship to work, so of course, I said, "okay." It took me several months to pack up all of our things, because I didn't want to just take everything we owned because our relationship was so back and forth that it became very difficult to know when he was gonna put us out again.

# "He Hits"

It was a Saturday, in the summer in the Sunshine State. I was enjoying life as much as I could but living on the edge of a breakdown. Everything was going fine, and we were getting along, until I wanted to go somewhere. I had done got myself and our daughter ready and I guess he did not like what I had on or either my hair was not to his liking. Either way, he says something to me about it and I blew it off. Because it was not that serious to me. Well, it was serious to him… I don't remember nothing but picking myself and my daughter up off the floor. I knew exactly what happened. I took our daughter to the back and I went in the bathroom and cried. When I came out of the bathroom, I did not say a word to him. I knew that I had to get out of this as quietly, but as quickly as possible. I did not want to make him any angrier than he already was. Once I got myself together, I went and got our daughter and got her ready for bed, put her to sleep and did the same for myself. When I woke up the next day, I waited until he left to go to work and packed all of our things and went back to my mother's house. When I got there, my mother did not ask any questions, just welcomed us with open arms.

I did not take his calls for a few days. I needed him to forget about me and just focus on our daughter because whatever we had was completely over at this point. Forget about that fairytale shit, I was done! After a couple weeks, I decided to take his call. He invited me over and of course I had our daughter in tow. He wanted to talk… I agreed to go. "Why did I agree to go?" It was dead silence on the ride there. I did not have nothing to say. When we got there, he had dinner cooked. We ate and he talked. He apologized. I accepted it. "Why did I accept his apology?" We put our daughter to sleep and ended up sleeping together… "What in the hell was I thinking?" I should have run for the hills and stayed away. But he was very convincing, and I thought he was really sorry for doing what he did. Even with this happening, the good still outweighed the bad, and that was the way I saw it. What can I say?! He was my daughter's father.

# "SURPRISE...
# SHE'S A BEAUTY"

W̶e were doing great and all was well in the universe. At this point we were still engaged. I was approached by someone that were having a Valentine's Day Banquet that knew both him and me and knew we were engaged. (Oh yeah, he proposed back when I was in high school, but it wasn't significant that's why I didn't expound on it). She asked if we wanted to have our wedding ceremony at the Banquet. I talked to him to see how he felt about that, he was cool with it. We wouldn't have to do much planning; they would handle everything except our wardrobe. It was perfect for me because I did not want a big wedding. I just wanted my twin sister to be in it. We already knew what the color would be. Both of our favorite color is red, and it was Valentine's Day so that was easy. Now to find me, my daughter, and my sister a dress. We found my daughter's dress first. And let me just tell you, her dress was so beautiful. It had a little bonnet to go with it. Just adorable! Ruffles all over and it was pure white. Her dress set me back a bit, but it was so worth it. She was my flower girl and my nephew was the ring bearer. My sister's dress was red, form fitting with sequin at the top. My dress was simple, his mother spruced it up by adding rhinestones to it and as well as the veil. It was decent but did not cost half as much as our daughter's dress. I did not have much money, so I was not trying to spend a lot of it on a dress and plus to be completely honest, I wasn't for sure we were making the right decision.

We went along with it anyway. And when it was Valentine's Day, that evening… we did it. We got married. The whole thing was a surprise to our families. My mother, my father, some of our family, friends and people that we didn't even know were in attendance. We were married by his stepfather who was an Elder. We went through the whole ordeal; the counseling beforehand was the main one that I remember. Him and I were totally different people and at that time it didn't resonate that this would be a major issue. I also did not think that I would learn so much from it.

After the wedding I was all set to just go home, because we had not made plans to do anything else. But he had a surprise for me, and he ended up getting a hotel and we stayed the night there. We were so tired from the running around and making sure everything was good for the evening that I don't even remember that night. I do, however, remember my prom night in which he was also my date.

I think we only stayed there one night and went home the following day. But I could be wrong. Anyway, we were happy and getting along really well at this time. I was working at a grocery store and he had been on his current job for a while at this point. He depended on his earnings to pay the major bills, my money was basically for the small bills, my bills, which I did not have but maybe one, and the upkeep of our daughter, I was not making much.

While working at the grocery store, I did not have a set scheduled and would work in the mornings, days and even nights. However, I did not work overnight. One morning I woke up to get ready for work I found myself hovering over the toilet. This happened for a few days, like clockwork every morning. I did not know what it could have been. I went to the clinic and found out I was pregnant. I didn't know how to react when the nurse came and told me the results... I was not happy. I remember her expecting a different reaction as she knew I was a newlywed. I wanted to be happy, I really did! But all I could think about is how am I going to financially take care of another kid. Even though I was married, I did not know how long that would last and I would have to take care of these kids all by myself if I got a divorce. I know that is negative, but as you've read up until this point, I don't have luck when it comes to happiness, something or someone always seems to come in and snatch the little bit of happiness I might have. Eventually, I got excited because she was a HIGHLY active little bundle in my stomach. She did not let me relax at night, she was a night owl, just like her father. She was so bubbly; I didn't have a choice but to get excited about her nine-month journey. When we counted the months, we found out that I, for a fact got pregnant before the wedding, so in reality both of our daughters were in our wedding. This made me smile! I know it may seem small to you, but this was huge to me, I do not know why, but I was excited to find that out. It did not take me long to start showing. I mean it seemed that as soon as I found out, my stomach started poking out. I wanted to keep it somewhat of a secret cause I didn't want people trying to figure out that I was pregnant before our wedding. It was none of their business. But I knew somebody would make it a big deal. That is just how it was where I am from.

The nine months took forever. You couldn't tell me that I wasn't pregnant for more than nine months, because I would call you a "storyteller". It was at my baby shower, which I was told that you should have a baby shower for the first baby only, when I announced to our families who the god mother would be, which was one of his cousins. She gladly accepted and I love her forever for it.

A couple of weeks or so later I started having contractions. I started watching the time in between the contractions. The doctor said, "go to the hospital when the contractions are five mins apart". Well, first of all I still had a few more days before my due date, and I did not want to chance having our baby on my father's birthday as I wanted her to have her own special day. Also, I remember that from the first time and I did exactly as I was told, I felt I was in the hospital too long before I delivered. I didn't want to go through that again because I hated hospitals. Therefore, I waited until they were about three minutes apart. Bad idea. Reason is, I had already told the doctor at one of my appointments that I would make the decision if I wanted to get an epidural when I came to the hospital on delivery day. He said that I would have time to make the call then, because I was unsure if I wanted to get this injection. I was trying to convince myself that if I felt the pain that I would think twice about getting pregnant again. Although I do not regret my daughters, I never wanted kids, at least not until I got my life together. I got to the hospital too late to be offered the injection. They were in rush mode to prep me. I had to give myself an enema, I remember having to do that in the bathroom down the hall from my birthing room. Once that was done, the pain was so severe I could hardly walk by myself. He did come in the bathroom and offered to help with the enema. I refused as I had already did it. He helped me to the room. He was still such a gentleman when it came to most things. No soon as I got in the bed to get comfortable, the enema started working… I was ready! I tried to go as fast as I could so I would not shit myself… I made it! LOL… What a relief. I did not know how he would have felt had I shitted down that hallway. I am just saying, he probably would have been embarrassed, because I sure would NOT have. "It is what it is". It is just life and somethings in life you cannot control. I ended up giving birth an hour before my father's birthday. I was ecstatic! I had reached my goal! Seems simple, but in our family birthdays are huge. It is the only holiday you have to yourself, for people to celebrate you. We welcomed another baby girl! She was perfect! And I did my run down... I checked for two arms, two legs, ten fingers, and ten toes... then I checked facial to make sure she was as perfect as I knew she would be. And she was! When my six weeks was up, I went back to working at the grocery store. But I needed to find a way to make more money, because now there were two. I did get WIC to help with stuff for them and breastfeeding them both helped quite a bit. Except this lil one did not take well to the breast. It was very painful when she latched. She was rough and greedy as hell. I ended up pumping into bottles for her.

I put in applications just about everywhere. It was hard for me to get an interview. But once they met me in person, I knew I would get the job. My resume at the time was not as great because I did not really know how to write one and did not have much to put on it as my experience was very minimal. I started working for this family owed company. That specialized in insurance and bail bonds. I really loved this job and the folks that owned it was really good to me. I gravitated to them really quick. I was there for maybe a year when one of my coworkers moved on to a better job and her position opened up. The position was making like fifty cents more than what I was making. The boss asked me if I wanted it, I did not hesitate. I was so excited. It was better for them to hire from within as I had knowledge and could do everything there. I was willing to do both until they got a replacement for me. I learned so much from them, which gave me the experience I needed to move up. But because this was a small business, there was no growth and in order to make more, I had to leave them altogether.

# "THE MILESTONE"

Once they advertised that there would be a GEICO being built in South Lakeland, I was all over it. I had worked in insurance and I had experience and shouldn't have a problem getting the job. At least that was my thought process at the time. They were having an open house and was hiring people on the spot. I ended up skipping work to attend. I did not bother calling out because I just knew I was going to get the job.

However, I do regret not calling, because I left them in a bad spot and could not use them as a reference with all the experience I learned there. I learned in my older years to never do that again. And to always give your employers advance notice if you intend on leaving to give them time to replace you. I was still young and learning. Well I got the job. It was paying way more than I was making. The commute was longer, but the pay was so worth it. My hours were 2pm-midnight, Monday-Thursday. I loved this schedule. It worked well with our living situation too. He would go to work early in the morning, and I would have the girls then, and when I was ready to go to work, he would be getting home, and he would take the night shift. It worked out, until my hours were changed. They completely got rid of that shift. And I had to choose another shift. With the shifts available to me, it was clear that I would have to either put our daughters in daycare or get a babysitter. Day care was out of the question because I no longer lived in the same town. I had to find someone either in my family or his. We ended up asking his cousins (who will remain unnamed). They were great! They ended up being the only people that watched my daughters! This family have done so much for our daughters, I cannot thank them enough for everything. Saying "thank you" will never be enough for all they have done. The bond built and friendships made... I love the whole family!

Starting a new shift means getting a new supervisor and coworkers. I am a friendly person, so it wasn't hard for me to build bonds in the group since we were always in contests against other sections and had to basically work together to reach and surpass goals. At this time, I did not have my license to sign off policies even though I was selling the hell out of them. It was not required as the company would train you and then pay for us to get it. Well, the time had come for our section to go and get our license. What I knew about insurance was very minimal compared to the shit they had on the test. The reason is the test was broad and cover the entire spectrum of insurance. I only worked in a particular section and that was all I knew. Let me set the scene… When you enter into the building, they direct you over to the photo section, you take your photo. I was so confident, you couldn't tell me that I wasn't about to ace this test, so when I took my picture, I smiled really big! Once the photo is taken you are then directed to go into this lil room to take the test. Now, every test is different as they are computer generated. Y'all when I tell you that I had never heard of half of that mess that was on that test. By the time I got halfway through I found myself saying "any, mini, miny, moe. Needless to say, I did NOT pass that day. Even though I was not the only one who did not pass in my group, I was bummed. But I knew what I had to do. I was not the type to let anything "beat" me. So, I got my study material and I studied day and night, in between calls and on break. It did not make no sense that this job is giving me this opportunity and I was not taking full advantage of it. My mother had taught me better.

The next test date was schedule. Even though I studied, I was not as confident as I was the first time. I was a little intimidated and that was out of character for me. But, because the tests were computer generated, I did not know what to expect. So, when we walked in, the photo op was blah, because I was so focused on the test. Well, after a little over an hour, I was ready to submit my test for grading. And to my surprise, I passed… I got ALL of the questions right! I was so happy! I had a feeling I would pass but did not want to jinx myself. Once you pass, you wait on your license. I was ready to take my photo again. But you do not get a chance to take another photo and they use the one you took before you entered into the testing area. I was not happy, because I did not smile, and my picture did not reflect my real feelings. I was hesitant to show my license to my coworkers back at the building. But I did! They all understood the face.

There were about ten people in each section. I was the top seller on many occasions and the bonuses that we received were out of this world. I did not know what to do with this kind of money. We were never taught how to manage money. I messed over most of it. I can admit that. I messed over it so much that I told a story to my husband. At the time, I really needed to purchase something. I cannot remember if it was gas or something for the girls. All I know is that I really needed the money. See I had access to his checkbook, and he did not mind me writing checks when I needed something if I just let him know. Well, this particular day, I am not sure why I was afraid to ask him for the amount I really need. I think it was because I did not want him asking me why I didn't have any money or what I did with my money. So, I only asked him if I could write a check for five dollars. Five dollars was a safe number and would not make a difference, so it was safe. Well, he said, "yes". I ended up writing the check for fifty dollars! This was the first and last time I was untrue to my husband… it killed me. A couple weeks after, he approached me. He was not happy, because of course, his checking account was forty-five dollars short. He was the type to watch the money with a fine-tooth comb. I figured that if all the bills were paid that month, it would be alright. He wasn't mad about the money; he was upset that I told a story to him. I understood that and I felt really bad, which is the reason I was honest with him, if he asked me something, from this point on.

www.ingramcontent.com/pod-product-compliance
Lightning Source LLC
Chambersburg PA
CBHW061635050726
47502CB00012B/2239